THE ELIMINATION GAME

Mary Mulholland's poems are widely published and regularly mentioned in competitions. Former psychotherapist, with a Newcastle/Poetry School MA in Poetry, she founded the platform Red Door Poets and is an editor of *The Alchemy Spoon*. She has a pamphlet from Live Canon and two collaborations from Nine Pens with Vasiliki Albedo and Simon Maddrell. Occasionally she can be found looking after 300 Barbados Blackbelly sheep in the West Country. www.marymulholland.co.uk

Also by Mary Mulholland

What the sheep taught me   (Live Canon, 2022)

CONTENTS

ISBN: 978-1-917617-21-5

Cover designed by Aaron Kent

Cover art: © okalinichenko / Adobe Stock

Edited and Typeset by Aaron Kent

Broken Sleep Books Ltd
PO BOX 102
Llandysul
SA44 9BG

the elimination game

Mary Mulholland

Broken Sleep Books

GROWING A FACE

years back i'd count how long
old people would pause before
they could answer a question,
skin falling in folds as they spoke,
eyes watery, marked in red pen.
i'd wonder why they grew so bent,
as if trying to touch the ground,
why they sat so long, had they lost
the will to run, why they didn't open
windows, what they still found fun.
once i asked great aunt maude why
she drew lines on her face. she laughed.
once workmen whistled and called,
cheer up, love, might never happen.

VIBURNUM HAIKUS

cupid's arrow-shaft
pierced a bronze age mummy's heart
caused the ice to melt

unexpected love
can awake the longest dead
the oldest woman

pink white cream flowers
see her waving bare tree arms
pliable in cold

her bright red berries
her honey scent and sweet bark
startle you awake

WOODSTOCK
after Jitish Kallat

Tomorrow I'm going back to Yasgur's farm:
smoking grass, music flattening trees,
whale-sound, cinnamon candles

and a kohl-eyed girl in a purple kaftan,
flowered peace-band circling long hair.
Cross-legged she sits among beautiful people

half a million strong.
Did they all become accountants?
I turn pages and pages of the battered journal,

even my writing has changed. Last week
at the Biennale, I stood in a doorway, in words
projected onto mist: *Become who you are,*

but just as songs rocked a town, I contain multitudes.
Tomorrow we're off to find one we left behind.

THE GENERAL'S WIDOW

The world sees only her public look,
pearls and smiles, but when he dies
she locks the door and busies herself
on their once-shared bed, now covered
with a pink satin spread. She's making
a cast of her husband's head, paints it
red to adorn the mantelshelf, replace
those snaps of his sons and 'himself'.

Later she smells his cigars in the air
as she sits at noon in his fireside chair,
contemplating her scarlet masterpiece.
The funeral's over, it's such a relief,
she'll spend the night making paper planes,
hurl them at his eyes, nose and brains.

BEARD

With the air of an empress she glides by,
her smile apologetic, and her chin –

think Lowry. His train journey, Manchester
to Paddington. In his compartment a hirsute lady,
whom he drew discretely until she, distressed,
asked this shy man what he was doing.

Lowry later claimed he and the woman,
'intelligent and able, but completely alone
behind her deformity', parted as friends –
then sold it as one of his 'sordid Lowries'.

Yet think: De Ribera's breastfeeding mother.
Think, the Sphinx, though hers was epilated.
Think, too, Hatshepsut, first female pharaoh,
her postiche kept in place with gold ribbon.

THE ELIMINATION GAME

grey hat   silver car   middle lane
long in the jaw noachian out of the
(b)ark winter chicken over the hill
perch-clinging   rocking the bridge
unhipped & cankered batty old trout
shadow-unsewing   moth-eaten
goose with a sole mother-wit future
of will-rewriting   &   FU for the
shoehorning   kindly wait while i
find a bucket to list & puke in   this
is my time of horse-sense   & grey-
beard   my inner-peace search   let
me tell you   last year i swam in the
arctic   trekked the sahara   then
mastered roller-blading   next up
i'm starting classes in mandarin

HOTWATER BOTTLE

For Christmas my daughter gave me
a warm hug, covered in grey felt,
with my initial in Liberty print.
I can see her even stitches, the crease
between her brows as she focused
her scarred brown eyes – refused
to be scared by patches and fireworks
if she could see like other people.

Nose to paper when young, she'd breathe
in Jane Austen, Jilly Cooper, Agatha Christie,
the space between pages, absorbed a world
where people pruned the roses.

She says when I'm old she wants me to live
with her and the roses. Tenderly she'll place
a plaster on my skin torn by a thorn,
cover my head with a sunhat while I rest
on a deckchair, as she dries rose petals
and makes lavender bags to bring on sleep.

HELL HOLE (*KOLLHELLAREN*)

friends say surely she's too old to swim
in the arctic, but the cold at å takes her
back to childhood, and she likes that

here people don't smile much,
midsummer mountains snow-topped,
maelstroms only for the brave and bold.

here a thin crust holding the earth
slowly pushes and folds until it tears,
the way skin is plastic to time and change.

here the coast is ravaged by elements.
she's on a small boat outside a dark cave,
others on board all half her age,

though inside she still feels thirty.
she knows she must enter the hell hole
in a no-seeing, feeling-way forward

along passages that endlessly branch.
and she is one of the red-oxide figures
running on walls, where they've been running

thousands of years in faceless search,
but she's also the dog that got lost,
emerged weeks later, trembling, hairless,

with wild eyes and turning in circles,
unable to stop grappling with the dark.
as if all searching leads to a room

filled with impenetrable riddles.

ROLE CHANGE

your hand is miniature in mine.
i run my finger over the wrinkled skin

of your body, afraid
to hold you, a quarter my genes,

your eyes shut fast like a puppy
exhausted after a long journey.

they point out a tiny black tear
falling from your pupil, but

it may help you see through dark times.
swaddled in cream, you wriggle and stretch,

supple as a yogi, then snuggle close.
i adjust the wrap. my lips brush your down,

feel the pulse of life in your fontanelle.
my fingers like sandpaper as i prise

open your fist. i want to find strong lines
of life, love and fate –

i know they're there.
but you wrap your fingers around mine,

hide your palm, clutch me tight.
so tight, i can lift you, dangling.

GRANDMOTHER'S FOOTSTEPS
palinode to Patricia Lockwood's homage to 'Ode on a Grecian Urn'

Of course they welcome the urn. With *breath*
like horse medicine, violets in hats and all that
forgetfulness, the old long for death
to all sorts of things. I shut the book, turn

again to James from the Arts Council talking
to a roomful of ladies the age of his mother,
he recommends we kickstart projects, step-
change careers, champion diversity, we should

all be applying for funds. He meets my eye,
makes me believe anything's possible.
Even for urn-waiting crones
reciting their poems to empty halls.

One died recently, started late, in marketing
terms, out-of-date. Left four hundred poems,
unpublished, many good; isn't there beauty
in small truths, too? James says find a new audience.

I could give creative classes at the local junior,
poetry is horse medicine for the soul. I'll apply
for funds for *Grandma's Footsteps,* photocopy
the grant, stuff it in an urn, and post it to Patricia.

TRAPPIST

she's walking away from her collection of feathers,
sparrow, wren, white-tailed eagle, she has enough

to impress the flying monk of Malmesbury, she's leaving
behind her six Cream Legbars, their blue eggs,

abandoning raincoats, and other forms of protection,
her habit of joining but not belonging to crowds.

she's turning her back on dreams and other dark matters,
relinquishing further attempts to help in family affairs,

she's given away her jewels, silver vaults, wine cellars,
returned bank cards, sold her car,

made legal provisions for the future, chosen hymns,
imagined the party, she's had her fill of parties.

she's heading to an anechoic chamber, where she'll live
with silence, cloud divination.

CROISSANTS

We eat snails under the lime tree,
my daughter, her family and me,
but they move too fast, jump
from *l'expo* to *l'environnement*.
Now she's French we don't often speak
the same language.
I clench my hands, focus on the wasp
trap hanging from a branch. Wings bent,
one crawls down the bottleneck.
They ask if I'm praying. I join in
the laughter. A crescent moon rises.
The six-year-old says she hears bats,
and the children are taken complaining to bed.
Perhaps even children find it hard to be children.
The swing falls still. Overnight
the trampoline will fill with leaves.
Tomorrow I'll get croissants from the *boulangerie*.
I scrape candlewax from the table,
blow out the light.

PIETÀ

Crows know the mystery of life, they don't sing
lullabies yet form loving families, grieve

at funerals. A crow once landed on me.
It flapped its wings, a black fan at my face.

It's not only the moon that has a dark side,
even Labradors can transform a walk into a snarl.

Photography is a cheap trick to make things last.
People are like clouds, shifting,

on storm days they turn purple.
In *The Modification of Clouds,* Luke Howard

gave them names, *cumulus, cirrus, stratus.*
Son of a lampmaker, he corresponded

with Goethe, Constable, Ruskin; everyone
now noticed clouds, tried to hold onto them.

When I held my newborn, the Lab barked
and wagged his tail. But I saw an image of the *pietà,*

as if knowing that day would come.
How a mother's nights are lit with prayer, her ceiling

of crows, wanting her child to be happy, learning
what this entails. I still chant from *Carmina Gadelica*,

there are so many kinds of death. I cradled my baby,
and people thought I was crying for joy.

MY PEOPLE WERE CHIEFTAINS

Once my people were rulers and emperors
we were the wise ones, revered, respected.
Elders and betters.

My people spoke in strong voices
everyone heard. Now if we tell stories
the public is bored and call us

a shuffle of wandering fog people
who got it wrong. Wrong our values,
our driving and child-rearing, wrong our treatment

of natural resources, my people ruined the world,
we are history, our gifts unwanted.
If we try our hands at poetry or art, that's best

left to the young. Our time is done.
If we wear make up, keep up in fashion
we're mutton, if seen dancing, making love on a carpet

my people are scorned, we are shamed,
skin loose on our bones is our preparation.
My people remind you: one day this will be you.

FALLEN TREE

The airplane, the vast oak brought down
in a storm, is where the grandkids run to
when they visit, dragging me by a hand.

I'm pilot down the runway of the drive,
we soar over the white horse on the plains,
gain altitude. I chat about those who've passed
until the eldest cries, *There's Great-Granny
Dodo*, or *Great-Grandpa Bob*. And we swoop
in as a young woman from the colonies
boards a ship to Southampton. A redhead
parachutes behind German lines. Now they're
meeting at a dance, bombs explode like fireworks.
Bob, even younger, pulls dace from the Nene,
Dodo's a child in cane-fields with a pet monkey.

Next I'll tell them about their own father,
how he sailed the Fastnet, skied off-piste,
raced his car two hundred miles an hour,
living out the label of his first bike,
a green Raleigh, *always more extreme*.

I won't tell them what it's like to be thrown about
by thermals, lost in cloud, having to switch on radio
navigation, search for landing sensors.
The youngest will stick his arm out, but
no one's behind.

Yet one day they'll come, the grandchildren.
I'll show them the plane, talk about birds
that don't fly, sheep that loudly graze, that fallen
trees sometimes right themselves.

READING THE SILENCE

The sound of the sea is his breathing,
they sit without talking either side
of a fire. A rustle as his finger slides
down paper, turns a page.

Rain lashes the panes, rattled by wind,
the shrill cry of an owl,
while in here a fly as if drunk buzzes
and bumps round the lamp.

He rises, swats the fly into the fire,
adds a log. An explosion of sparks
on the carpet. He stamps them out,
refills his glass, returns to his reading.

Once in Africa, with rain like steel drums
on the tin roof, he said whisky was safer
than water, and the grey parrot, once owned
by a bronchial old man, coughed.

She pauses her knitting, replays her thoughts,
plain, purl, clacketing needles, perhaps time
to cast off. She glances. He raises an eyebrow,
she half-smiles.

WHY I'M SIGNING UP FOR PSYCHO-TANGO

music comes from the bandstand in the park
posters on trees advertise dance as therapy

sometimes i regret not learning the tango
betjeman said he regretted not having more sex

most men i meet are impotent by sixty
it's the age people concentrate on close bonds

with dentists and doctors
my dentist holds me steady to enter my mouth

if i had the wisdom of trees i'd see sixty as young
the poster says tango's a conversation between bodies

psychoanalysis and tango twins of longing and desire
for connection   my foot taps to the music

i watch a man and woman   arms flung open
two strangers   walk towards each other

sway   lean close   pull away   reconnect
cross legs   sidestep   corkscrew   hold the gaze

it's starting to rain   they keep dancing

a white-haired man in a long blue coat shoots me
a glance *if you can walk you can dance   it's all slow*

slow quick quick slow   he says   slowly moves on
i hurry after   *shall we give it a go?*

THE GRANDMOTHERS

a cluster of parisian grandmothers
fakely blonde or black-haired
are elegantly chatting and laughing
a half-eye on their grandchildren
and the playground is full
of high-pitched *mamie* and *grandmère*

i'm digging nails into palms
following my child's children
scaling spider ropes designed for big boys
but they're not and they're at the top

i can see the little one falling
blood pouring eyes unblinking
the other grandmothers staring shocked
and me barely speaking their language

i want to ask if i came here daily
would i ease into role
or are they secretly stabbing palms
with their scarlet nails

i call to the boys *let's go*
and they fly off on scooters
narrow pavements   buses   car-horns
they're laughing   i'm running
then we're back   up six floors   no lift
supper   bath   endless stories
books mostly in french

i wake to their gentle breathing
what is the language of dreams
soon my daughter will open the door
a waft of cigarette-perfume-wine
she'll ask *did you have a fun time*
i'll say *yes everything was fine*

LITTLE DEATH

he's on the right

                    she's on the left
                    she turns her back
                    cross from their tiff
                    is drifting off when

he moves on top

                    she's not averse but

he's too quick then
with a grunt rolls back

                    his petite mort
                    & her waiting

he tosses & turns
sighs for an hour
says *indigestion*
goes down to make tea

                    it's 3 o'clock
                    she thinks of the link
                    men of his type
                    tiptoes down
                    expecting a corpse

he's on the sofa
most shades of grey

                    she takes him to a&e

connected to tubes
& monitors he hears
men of his age &
proudly boasts
what brought it on   as if she's not here
            & the female doctor
            says he'd have died
            had he delayed
            coming

THE REGRETTING ROOM

i hang up my scar-coat

things consumed to avoid the consequences of feeling

things i can't remember

books i took for the taking

the text i wrote at two when i gave up waiting

a photo-shoot appointment i missed in new york

the *yes* i couldn't say to your face

three lovers i roped together

my dark shades that stop me speaking

my inability to feel without using a blade

the shadows and shadows and shadows

that night I didn't call my mother but went to a film

by morning she was dead

the colour of wrongdoings is a night without moon

in this room i find a child who hid long ago –

ask if she's willing to swap places

it's full-moon again time. before i die
i'll have seen one thousand. should i count

life in moons. call myself blood. call myself wolf.
call myself blue. years won't make me revered.

yet she is never witch-mooned. crone-mooned.
not decried as unstable when she is

edging away at the speed fingernails grow.
she's not in second childhood. third age.

as if it's an illness to reach three score and ten.
'dear'. drugged. dumpy sofa. a tree to be felled.

if old people are 'othered' does it make us
a different species. hearts have green energy.

last night i was picking oranges. this is a dream
of tears and anxiety. i've reached the waiting room

filled with the half-alive. threshold to a terrain
all fear to enter yet as rich with possibility

as the challenger deep. the elders' luminous
adventure. if we use all our eyes like stargazers.

ACTS IN THE MAKING

- elders were planted by houses as protection

- a baby in her pram studies branches
- a toddler sets off alone into a desert
- a child stares out at other children
- a seven-year-old is bullied by a boy she likes

- a teenager stops eating at family mealtimes
- a thin teenager gives up talking
- a twenty-something hides in the Carnevale di Venezia
- a thirty-something has a mask for every occasion

- a forty-something is lost in the tail of a forest
- she confesses to a priest she doesn't believe in love
  and he absolves her with a kiss
- an old woman in There And Back Again Lane sees
  elder berries ripening black leaves

IF TODAY WERE CIRCLED IN RED

maybe you'd sit up and see who's hiding
the way humans play with secrecy & forgetting
the banishing properties of certain trees
you'll rise like a reinvented teenager
shout at a river pausing in its flow
search for fragments of your face at an 88 bus-stop
suspended
reach for a helium balloon shaped like a rose
drape cherries on your ears even if no one eats them
they're all busy listening to 'revolution 9' on a loop
& you won't care that hopscotch has no answer
why sixpences are exiled to museums & plum puds
or why you lost the letter from your mother
but not the money she sent & before running out
of time you'll give up walking backwards in galoshes
as if life were just a fold in the paper
& another

FRANTUMAGLIA

Mottled sleep by day, and nights
are expansive, he's back on route 66,
open-top Cadillac with wings to reach
the canyon's other side. He'd do it now.
And that trippy girl who tried to butterfly
to the heart of the canyon. The air still

carries her scent, this merciless air.
How he howled his way home, couldn't
stop her, but life carries on, he's carrying
on – cuffs frayed, skin yellowed, teeth
that prefer ice-cream and soup.
He turns from children laughing

outside the window, catches himself
in the convex mirror above the fire,
shrunken, silent, in uniform, he's watching
old people sip sherry, discuss the cold
war and government ministers,
as if the world belonged to them alone.

*frantumaglia is a dialect Neapolitan word defined by
Elena Ferrante as a heterogeneous mix of thoughts*

STILLING TIME

when she turned eighty my aunt refused to go
to bed, *because that's where most people die.*

at eighty eleanor of aquitaine rode on horseback
like a man when she went to visit the king of spain.

a woman even older circumnavigated the world,
another ran marathons, one wrote racy books.

when i'm eighty i'm going to retrace my steps
to the grand canyon, breathe again the air

where i first encountered the majesty of creation.
i will touch a black stone ninety million years old

and feel young. i'll bump into a family of elk
at dawn, we will hold each other's gaze.

i'll tell them i come in peace, leave my shadow
falling over the canyon edge, sinking into earth.

ACKNOWLEDGEMENTS

Some poems in this pamphlet have already been published and I'd like to acknowledge the following magazines and anthologies where they first appeared: *AMBIT, Momaya anthology, Marble, InkDrinkers, IamInPrint, Hippocrates Anthology, bathmagg, Drawn to the Light, Winchester Competition Anthology* and *Under the Radar*.

All my thanks to Aaron Kent and his fantastic team at Broken Sleep Books for making this possible, and to all my poet-friends, you know who you are, particularly Red Door Poets and The Circle, who helped on drafts of these poems, and never forgetting my wonderful family for their support and belief in me.

LAY OUT YOUR UNREST